INDEPENDENCE

WHY SCOTS SHOULD RULE SCOTLAND

ALASDAIR GRAY

CANONGATE

Royalties from the
sale of this book go to
Clydeside Action Against Asbestos
a registered charity
15 St Margaret's Place
Glasgow G1

First published in 1992
by Canongate Press plc
14 Frederick Street, Edinburgh EH2 2HB

British Library Cataloguing in Publication Data
A record is available in the British Library

ISBN 0–86241–391–5

Typeset by Falcon Typographic Art Ltd,
Fife, Scotland
Printed and bound in Scotland by
Courier International, East Kilbride

Contents

Author's Note

This pamphlet omits many important things: an independent Scottish education now almost destroyed by British government action; Scotland's usefulness as a separate testing ground for laws later enforced in England (extra police powers, the poll tax) and much else. This cannot be helped in a short phamplet which I think of as a sketch for a bigger picture to be completed before 2000 AD – if I am spared.

A G

CHAPTER 1

The Scots and Where They Come From

The title of this book may sound threatening to those who live in Scotland but were born and educated elsewhere, so I had better explain that by Scots I mean everyone in Scotland who is able to vote. Many folk who feel thoroughly Scottish live and vote in England, America or Hong Kong: but this book is about Scottish government so lumps them with Scots below the age of eighteen. Their lives and opinions are important, but outside the argument. My definition cheerfully includes many who think themselves English but work here as hoteliers, farmers, administrators and directors of Scottish institutions: also those who live in Scotland because they could buy a pleasant house more cheaply here than in the south. My definition also includes a small but important group of Scots who mainly live or work elsewhere: great landowners like the Duke of ***** and Lady ***** of ***** who have homes and property in several nations but return to their ancestral home to shoot, hold family parties and vote; also the seventy-one Scottish members of parliament whose working days are almost wholly spent in London so have to live there too.

Some may think this definition of a Scot both too liberal and too narrow, but I believe every adult in a land should have equal say in how it is ruled so therefore belongs to it, however recently she or he arrived. The first people who called themselves Scots were immigrants.

The first Scots were a set of Irish invaders who settled in Argyllshire while the English were invading and settling in the south-east part of Britain. Through centuries of fighting and rubbing along beside the Pictish clans to the east of them and the Strathclyde Britons to the south the Scots gave their name and a king to these other countries. This king did not rule the far north, which was dominated by Norway, or the

rich farming country south of the Forth which had been
conquered by English-speaking Northumbrians who made
Edinburgh their northern capital. By now seven little nations
occupied the country called England: nine if we include the old
British nations of Cornwall and Wales. Then in 1028 England
was unified by the Danes. King Canute had turned the North
Sea into a Scandinavian lake; he ruled the east coast from
Norway down to Jutland, the west coast from Canterbury
up to Edinburgh. When the Danish empire (like all military
empires) suddenly collapsed, Scotland and England were left
within something like their present boundaries – the Scots had
taken over Northumbria north of the Tweed.

In those days and for centuries after the great mass of
the Scottish people spoke Gaelic and Anglo-Saxon was only
spoken in Lothian, the lands between Forth and Tweed. These
lands were the richest and most fertile so English invaders
always attacked through them. Edinburgh Rock was an easily
defended foundation for a capital city and beside the Firth of
Forth, a beautiful port for dealings with Europe. For these
three reasons the Scottish rulers mostly worked in the English
speaking part of their nation and came to use the language of
its natives.

The free and independent kingdom of Anglo-Saxony lasted
twenty years. In 1066 William the Bastard made it part of a
Norman empire on both sides of the English Channel. The
English nobles and squires tried to break away in a series
of revolts in the north helped by their former enemies the
Welsh, the Danes and the Scots. William was too strong and
smart for them. He bribed the Danes to keep away then went
into the north and burned towns, villages and farms, carefully
destroying harvests, cattle and agricultural tools so that famine
would kill the survivors. Some fled over the border to Scotland.
The north never troubled him again. Half a year later the
sixty miles north of York was still unpeopled desert. William
was now free to turn England into a feudal state dominated
absolutely by himself. The Anglo-Saxons who escaped blended
with the south part of Scotland. One of them married Malcolm,
the Scottish king, whose Celtic wife had just died.

In 1124 Scotland got a very soldierly king, David I, who had helped the Norman French with one of their civil wars. He was on the losing side but did not suffer for it and was so impressed by the Norman-French military organization that he gave Scottish estates to some of their nobility. That is how the feudal system started to replace the Scottish clan system. The great-great-grandson of one such noble became King Robert the Bruce.

Centuries passed before we had another wave of immigrants – the country was too poor to attract people from more fertile lands. The invasion of Edward I two centuries later and Oliver Cromwell three centuries after him billeted English soldiers in Scottish towns but hardly any of them married and remained: the first being too hotly hated, the second preferring their own country. Sometimes big Scottish landowners, annoyed by the quality of the local cloth, paid the families of Flemish weavers to come here and gave them small villages. Thankerton, Crawfordjohn, Symington and Pollokshaws began that way. No other lasting influx of settlers came here before the 19th century. By 1860 the railway network put the Scottish Highlands within a day's journey of south Britain, and following the example of Queen Victoria's Balmoral several rich Englishmen bought estates in the Highlands where land and native servants could be got almost as cheaply as in India. But perhaps these should not count as Scots since most of them had town houses in London and other country houses in England, where they usually voted.

In 1846 the Irish potato crop failed. Nearly a million starved to death, a million and a half saved their lives by going elsewhere, and for those who could not afford the fare to America the nearest ports were Liverpool and Glasgow. Their cheap labour greatly increased the size, industry, poverty and wealth of these two cities, but especially Glasgow. By the end of the 19th century it boasted of being the second richest city in the British Empire and was certainly a major port. Jews made homeless by pogroms in Russia and Poland came to Scotland as well as to England and America.

In the 20th century four successive waves of immigrants

arrived in Scotland. Like the Jews they can be numbered in hundreds rather than thousands. First came Italians from Tuscany where a disease had destroyed the grape vines. It was they who gave most native Scots their first experience of café life, ice-cream and fish and chips. Around 1960 came Indians and Pakistanis who mostly set up small grocery shops and restaurants selling their national food; shortly after these came the Chinese who are almost exclusively in the restaurant business. Foreign restaurants are an essential part of Scottish social life since restaurants which serve Scottish foods (beef, venison, pheasant, salmon et cetera) can only be afforded by the rich. Lastly came the English, drawn north by the greater spending power of their money here, or by lack of opportunities at home, or by marriage. It is not easy to discover figures for them but I think it safe to say that they outnumber all former immigrant waves, except the Irish. They are a completely different breed from the wealthy manufacturers who bought up Highland estates in the Victorian age. I mentioned them in my first paragraph: hoteliers, farmers, administrators and directors of our national institutions, and my friend Stephanie Wolfe Murray, director of Canongate Press, publishers of this book. It is meant for all who live and vote in Scotland, people I therefore regard as fellow Scots.

According to *Chambers Twentieth Century Dictionary* racism is "race hatred, rivalry or feeling: belief in inherent superiority of some races over others, usually with implication of a right to rule." Since nobody will read a writer who seems superior to them or tries to boss them I am terrified of being thought a racist, and hope I have cleared myself of that suspicion by demonstrating that the Scots are composed of many races, not one. Moreover, this pamphlet also deals at points with the English, French, Irish and Welsh, and I think does so without prejudice.

But a picture of Scotland as a pool filled by waves of incomers is false if it omits how Scots continually splashed into other countries. The following contents list shows where I do so.

CHAPTER 1: The Scots and Where They Come From – this introduction.

CHAPTER 2: The Scottish Difference – how a geology and landscapes made people living on them separate from the English, and created Europe's first nation state.

CHAPTER 3: A Kind of Freedom – Scottish culture compared with English from the *Declaration of Arbroath* to the *Satire of the Three Estates*.

CHAPTER 4: Another Kind of Freedom – how English foreign policy broke an old culture and invented a new kind of soul.

CHAPTER 5: Emigrants – Scottish emigrés from the first Crusade through the first King of All Britain to the inventor of the Bank of England.

CHAPTER 6: More Emigrants – from the Darien settlers to the first North British MPs.

CHAPTER 7: Highland Disaster, Lowland Recovery – the most complex chapter.

CHAPTER 8: Democracy – from the American War of Independence through many British Reform Bills and Parliaments until now.

CHAPTER 9: The Scottish Archipelago – a Frenchman's view among some personal memories.

CHAPTER 10: Sorts of Future – reasons why an independent Scotland will not be attended by every advantage those who want it would like, and why we need it all the same.

Since I argue that Scotland should have a strong government elected by its people this pamphlet is propaganda for the Scottish National Party, or for candidates of other parties who have declared for such a government without swithering from side to side on the matter. *Chambers Twentieth Century Dictionary* says propaganda is "any activity for the spread of opinions and principles, especially to effect change or reform"; so all political systems use propaganda and democracy depends on it. Yet even honest propaganda of the non-Goebbels sort tends to use clichés and rhetorical exaggerations. These can simplify an argument and make it more exciting for a while, but in the long run I agree with what Talleyrand said – anything exaggerated is irrelevant. In my effort to avoid rhetoric and give a broad-minded instead of single-minded argument I may sometimes sound too dry and factual. However, my publisher has promised to look over my shoulder and make suggestions if she thinks I am in danger of losing your interest.

CHAPTER 2

The Scottish Difference: A Dry Approach

The tersest description of how different kinds of land produce different kinds of people and government is in a lecture given by Patrick Geddes in 1923. He explained why the Chinese can only eat under a government which protects local communes and water boards; why the rich farmlands of Europe encourage government by competing markets; why emancipated heroines first appeared in 19th century Scandinavian literature; why Britain in the 20th century might come to look dirty and old-fashioned when compared with Norway and Sweden. He also describes the difference between two different kinds of farming, both found in every European nation. However, the difference between them is still the basic difference between Scotland and England.

The Poor Peasant

This is not the farm labourer or the ploughman, but the smallholder of the uplands. He occupies land better fitted for thorns and thistles than for oats and corn. Here labour, strenuous beyond all other, is needed; and wellnigh continuous throughout the seasons. Here economies are of the very essence of survival, storing for the winter and for seed and using both with frugal care.

There is an oft quoted verse in the Psalms, "They that sow in tears shall reap in joy. He that goeth forth and weepeth, bearing precious seed, shall doubtless come again with rejoicing, bringing his sheaves with him." Everyone understands quite literally this rejoicing at harvest. But one may ask learned Jew or Christian, alike in vain, to explain why the sower should be

11

described as weeping, or else get only metaphysical guess-explanations.

Whereas, here is the vividly pathetic reality of the early history of the poor peasant. Early forms of culture could seldom produce enough food for the year. So the institution of the season of Lent arose in the spring, as a time of blending the economic hardship with social discipline. See then this verse in its homely details: that of the poor peasant who must take the precious few grains that remain from the harvest store away from his children who are crying for food and from their starving mother. He strides out past them to the field with stern-set face. Yet when he has left them to cast the little store over the field, he too breaks down and weeps.

The poor peasant and his thrifty wife are compelled to more economy, foresight and saving than inhabitants of the gentler climate and better soil further down the valley. Hence the foundation of Banks and Insurance Companies has been initiated by this social type. Their surplus population also is constantly pressing down the valley and into the wider world, and, through its training – at once strenuous, frugal and provident – it succeeds exceptionally. Hence the frequent rise of men from this formation – Swiss, Scots or New England from familiar choice.

The Farmer

Pass on now to the richer peasant, upon the deep and fertile ploughlands of the plain that once was prairie: the farmer with his tall heavy-headed wheat that gives him his good white bread to eat and an ample surplus to sell. Here, with the ample crops, are better cattle and stronger horses, with all the time a normal surplus for better dwellings with pleasing gardens. In these lands a much greater population can be supported, so that instead of the isolated cottages we now find goodly villages and wealthy market towns – often,

in the old days, walled around and with substantial
gates.

The fact that Scotland was poor compared with England meant
that for centuries Scotland could not support a secure middle
class. Before the 18th century its cities were county towns by
English standards, its towns were villages, and the kings could
only rule with the help of clan chieftains, big landlords who
ruled their territory clannishly. Clannishness was enforced by
their fewness and wide dispersal as well as their poverty. Even
in the Lowlands the fertile strips along rivers were divided then
by vaster moorlands than divide them now. Our characters are
shaped by the sort of houses we grow up in, but also by the
character of our neighbours. If the people next door loudly
intrude on us we will either shift house, grow grimly defensive
or intrude noisily back. The character and speech of the Scots
(character and speech cannot be separated) has since been
moulded as much by the English as the English have been
moulded by the French. The Anglo-Saxon kings had ruled
England through parliaments chosen by their free men and
serf-owning farmers, but the feudal rule imposed on them by
William the Waster after 1066 had nothing to do with civilian
choices. Those who crossed the Channel with William came
because he was a successful soldier who would divide England
with them if they made him king of it. Which happened. His
greatest captains got whole counties in which they took the
best estates and divided the rest between their men. Each
officer got a Saxon village or two which he controlled with
the help of his private soldiers. Thus England was ruled by
a self-perpetuating class of military landowners whose trade
union conferred with its boss, the king, in the House of Lords.
For four centuries this class schemed and battled to bring all
Britain and France under its power. They conquered Wales,
much of Ireland and, from 1296 to 1314, Scotland too.

The 1296 conquest by Edward I (called *Malleus Scotorum* or
Hammer of the Scots) was a feudal triumph. The liberation
eighteen years later was a clan or tribal triumph, the victory
of an ancient system over one more modern.

In Chapter 1 I mentioned how David I brought feudalism into Scotland by giving parts of it to Norman knights. It was natural for him to want some of the highly trained military power the European and English kings wielded. The incoming knights depended on him far more than did the chiefs of the big Scottish families. The Scottish monarchy got on so well with the incomers, intermarried with so many of them, that when King Alexander died without heirs in 1286 the strongest claimants to the Scottish throne were descendants of the Norman French. Though they bore such names as Umfraville, Comyn, Balliol and de Bruis, they were now certainly Scottish (Bruce, for example, had a Celtic mother and spoke Gaelic) but they were part-time Scotsmen with estates in England, and when visiting those they were subjects of King Edward. So they asked Edward to choose which of them should be Scottish king. He said he would do so if they promised he would be their overlord when they were in Scotland too. They agreed. He chose John Balliol, and that was the end of Scotland as an independent country until the Scottish people had time to react to the news. The arrival of English troops and tax-collectors in their royal castles and county towns angered the plebeians and small lairds. One of these was William Wallace, who led a resistance movement.

When Edward, to quell it, sent an army north the Scots barons (including Robert the Bruce) hurried to his support. They did not want to lose their English property. Many may have feared that a popular success would deprive them of their property in Scotland too. At any rate the English invaders, though aided by the Scots barons, were defeated by the Scottish Commons, despite the widespread slaughter of civilian men, women and children. Wallace was a good tactician who used to his advantage the geography which made Scotland poor – the wildernesses between fertile districts. With the help of the Scottish Church he became the official guardian of the Scottish kingdom in the absence of a rightful king, and corresponded with Europe over matters of trade.

But there were still English garrisons on Scottish soil, English invaders to be fought. In one battle he was helped by Robert the Bruce, who afterwards apologized to King Edward for his temporary fit of treason and promised not to do it again. English rulers often forgave treason and murder when committed by their own class, a charming trait which persists to this day. But Wallace was at last captured, taken to Westminster, condemned as a traitor to King Edward, gelded then tortured to death. It was now clear that if a strong Scottish baron broke with Edward and made a bid for the Scottish crown he would have popular support. The two strongest were Bruce and Comyn. Bruce murdered Comyn and had himself crowned King of Scotland six weeks later.

Eight years passed before the last English garrison fell and the invaders beaten at Bannockburn. English invasions, Scottish counter-attacks continued long after but by 1320 most Scottish barons had joined the Bruce and lost their English property. For the first time in a century and a half Scotland was being ruled by people who were completely inside it and owed their power, and knew they owed it, to the will of the commoners. This made Scotland the first European . . .

Publisher: (looking over author's shoulder) Are you not being too historical? Why should modern Scots think their mediaeval victory matters today?
Author: Because our Scottish MPs are in the same state as the Scottish barons when they had sworn allegiance to the English king.
Publisher: Please explain that.
Author: Bruce, Comyn, Balliol and the others accepted subordinate places in the court of Edward, Hammerer of the Scots, because it secured their places and incomes in England. They also trusted him to keep Scotland for them. He was overlord of England, Ireland, Wales and a lot of France – surely he could keep Scotland for them? He could not. The Scots Commons broke away. If the Scots barons had not joined the Commons they would have lost Scotland too.

Today many Scots MPs (chiefly Labour ones) have enjoyed good salaries for years by their attachment to Westminster Palace (sometimes called "the best club in London") in jobs which allow them cosy adjacent apartments. By supporting a Great British political system they have had to exercise their brains less (I suspect) than English MPs who are pestered, bullied and bribed by surrounding English constituents, deputations and the City of London . Since 1707 the work of Scottish MPs has only been strenuous when the *Scots inside Scotland* disturb the City of London. Which is now happening.

Publisher: But Scottish MPs like Donald Dewar and Tam Dalyell are nothing like Bruce and Douglas and the Scottish feudal overlords.

Author: (growing excited) Thank goodness! Modern fighters for independence use votes, not swords, and if Britain is a democracy the Scots will get independence through the ballot box. But imagine the feelings of our parliamentary overlords if they have to leave "the best club in London" and work for us in Edinburgh, surrounded by Scottish natives! The Danes, Dutch, Belgians and Swiss have smaller lands, the Danes, Norwegians and Finns smaller populations, but they are used to ruling themselves. The Scots have lost the knack; relearning it will cause painful upheavals; but unless we get it again –

Publisher: Please stop bellowing, you are resorting to rhetoric.

Author: Then let me develop the argument in the dry, historical way I had planned.

CHAPTER 3

A Kind of Freedom

The Bannockburn victory made Scotland the first European nation state – the first to have territorial unity under one king. Kings of France, Germany, Poland and Hungary ruled counties inside each other's kingdoms: counties whose ownership was passed about through dynastic marriage as much as warfare. The Scottish commoners who resisted England had forced their landlords to abandon their multinational estates and become Scottish. The novelty of this is shown in the Declaration of Arbroath, a letter from Scotland to the pope. In 1320 the pope was a Frenchman assisted by England, so he decided to excommunicate everyone in Scotland unless they took Edward II as their overlord. The reply was written by the Abbot of Arbroath on behalf of the "barons and freeholders and the whole community of the realm of Scotland". The nobles who signed were Lowland Scots, Norman French, chiefs of Highland clans with Scandinavian Earls of Orkney and Caithness.

The Declaration said that since ancient times the Scots had been free to choose their own kings; that this freedom, like all freedoms, was a gift of God; that if Robert Bruce were weak enough to swear allegiance to the English king they would dismiss him and choose someone else. This assertion of Scottish independence held good. England's monarchs still continued to call themselves rulers of Scotland, just as they called themselves rulers of France for centuries after losing France: but Scotland was fully independent until the sixth James Stuart of Scotland was invited to take Queen Elizabeth's place in 1603.

But were the Scots better off for being ruled by their own bosses rather than foreign ones? Happiness and freedom cannot be measured scientifically so we must hunt for clues in chronicles and poems.

In the 14th century Froissart, French chronicler of European chivalry, came to Scotland and was struck by the bad manners of the Scottish peasants. If a nobleman rode over a field the men who worked it screamed and yelled at him to get off. This does not prove Scotland was democratic. It proves the astonishment of the common people at an act of wasteful selfishness. These peasants supported their lairds and nobility out of crops which barely kept them and their families alive. They expected the ruling classes to at least not damage the fields, and protested when they did. They might not live freely, but they could speak freely, unlike the peasants of England and France whose lords had every right, in custom and law, to ride rough-shod and hawk and hunt over peasants' land without let or hindrance. In the statutes of the French nobility there was even a "Right of Plunder": this allowed the military class to grab poultry, pigs, grain et cetera from the peasants without paying for it when they were short of money.

English imperialism often forced Scotland and France into alliance, and French troops sometimes visited Scotland to invade England from the north. Few of them liked their uncouth allies. Two hundred hungry soldiers from one expedition tried to plunder a district of Scottish farmers who counterattacked and killed them. If this had happened in other lands it would have been treated as a peasants' revolt. The Scottish government of the day let it pass. The survivors of the expedition were given food and lodging in Edinburgh, but not allowed to return to France before they had paid a heavy bill for it. This persuades me that the common people enjoyed some of the freedom mentioned in the declaration of Arbroath. There is another reason.

Froissart, the son of a man who painted heraldic shields, sincerely loved what an Irishman has ironically called "the grandeur that keeps the world going", so the freedom of the Scottish peasants' speech struck him as barbarous. Free speech, however, is essential to great literature, which withers if confined to a single class of society. Since English literature clearly shows this I will give a quick sketch-map of it for comparison with the Scottish achievement.

English literature falls into three periods: Anglo-Saxon,

Middle English and Modern; each so divided from the rest by centuries of tyranny that they read like different languages. The literature of the Anglo-Saxons was heroic, various and stopped by the Norman Conquest. English kings, gentry, judges and schoolteachers used nothing but French; English literature only started again when rulers and ruled started talking the same language. This happened when the French, unbearably taxed by Plantaganet kings with a secure base in England, began fighting them off. To raise troops for a war lasting several generations England's rulers appealed to the patriotism of the common English people by talking to them in their own language.

Then the Black Death killed between a third and a half of the population. People of every rank died but the deaths of the labourers caused the biggest upheaval. The pool of unemployment which normally keeps wages down vanished. The workers struck for higher wages and had to be given them. Warfare and the building of cathedrals and palaces stopped. For the first time the English people were jolted into widespread public debates in which great lords, abbots, bishops, country squires, city financiers and town councils jockeyed for power from positions of something like equality. And English literature began again.

All the great works of Middle English literature were written between 1360 and the end of that century: *The Cloud of Unknowing*, *Gawain and the Green Knight*, Langland's *Piers Plowman*, the poems and tales of Chaucer, Wyclif's translation of the Bible, were written within forty years. So was *The Bruce*, the first epic poem in the Scottish vernacular, but just now I am talking about England. Great writing there stopped when free speech stopped. The Peasants' Revolt in 1381 gave the middle and upper classes a terrible shock. It was stimulated by a poll tax brought in to finance more war with France, but it also demanded an end to serfdom. The revolt was partly led by worker priests and student intellectuals from Oxford. After being bloodily suppressed a law was passed forbidding schools to teach reading and writing to the children of labourers. Everyone who preached in public had to be licensed by bishops. Owning Wyclif's English Bible became a crime for anyone not a bishop or nobleman. *Piers Plowman*, a popular poem which described corruption in every part of Church and state and lamented the hunger of the poor, was banned by act of parliament. A highly conservative bishop who had written books attacking any reforms in Church and state was compelled to burn them – "he had written of profound matters in the English tongue."

Between the death of Chaucer in 1400 and the plays of Christopher Marlowe in 1592 only one great writer used the whole range of the English language to write a book for all the English people – Tindale's translation of the Bible, on which the later ones are based. He had to go abroad to get it written and printed in his own tongue, even so spies of Henry VIII had him arrested, strangled and burned in 1536: yet four years later Sir David Lindsay's *Ane Pleasant Satyre of the Thrie Estatis* was publicly performed before the Scottish king, lords and commons. This verse play makes brilliant comedy of how a corrupt king, clergy and burgher class exploit John the Common Weal – the peasant farmer whose work supports them all, and has nobody to support him but Divine Correction, an angel sent by God. Langland's *Piers Plowman* had said this in a longer and far more Christian poem, yet his book was banned. Between Barbour's Bruce epic and Sir David Lindsay came *The Kingis Quair* by James I, the poems of Dunbar, Henryson's *Testament of Cresseid*, Gavin Douglas's translation of the *Aeneid*, Blind Harry's *Wallace*. In this period the population of England rose from less than three million to perhaps four. In the same period the population of Scotland could hardly have been a fifth of that. At least two thirds were Gaelic speakers, though many were bilingual. Those who wrote and read *Inglis* (as the Scottish form of speech was called) cannot have been many more than five or six thousand.

Several things allowed the turbulent little nation to add this wealth of imaginative poetry to European literature. Firstly, a tradition of verses sung and chanted by many who could not write at all. Every land in the world had that in those days. Secondly, kings and landlords and clergy who shared the folk tradition. A haughty ruling class who pride themselves on their superiority to common speech depend on a secure middle class to shut them off from it, a class Scotland never got till the 18th century. Before the Scottish kings grew rich by going to England they were too poor to wholly divide themselves from the misery – that is to say, the *language* of the peasant; so though Scotland was no democracy it was far more egalitarian than its far richer neighbours. But a speech and folk tradition freely shared by bosses and underlings cannot become great writing without a wide *education* – a Latin word which means "leading outward", or learning of other traditions. The Scots makers of fine writing knew Gaelic, for though Inglis had by this time spread through the Lowlands the Lowlanders did not yet pride themselves on their ignorance of the older British speech, and the king had a Gaelic poet laureate as well as the other kind. With the possible exception of Blind Harry they were all clergy or trained by clergy, so knew Latin. Apart from Blind Harry the minstrel they were courtiers or close relations of courtiers so knew French. They also knew the literature of England and had great respect for the genius of Chaucer.

And in music also these four different strains – Gaelic, Church Latin, French and English – mingled in Scotland to produce (my friend John Purser tells me) a uniquely . . .
Publisher: Listen, this is all very interesting, but is it telling the readers why the Scots should rule Scotland?
Author: Yes! It shows that a poor government need not stop a small independent country having a rich culture, and that a wealthy government does not always help the culture of a large one.

CHAPTER 4

Another Kind of Freedom

By mere omission I may have suggested the Scots were a nation of defiant peasants protected by popular kings; but Lowland peasants and Highland clansmen were under landlords and chiefs who were almost absolute kings on their own territory, and sometimes did atrociously criminal things to their underlings and each other. The English kings had at last controlled such people with the help of townsmen who needed some peace and steady justice to follow their trades, and paid taxes to the crown for it – even provided bands of armed citizens sometimes. Scotland's trade was so meagre and her towns so poor that in most the provost and magistrates were appointed by the big local landlord who collected the taxes himself. So to get some assistance against the barons the kings had built up the power of the Church with such big grants of land that at last the Church owned a third of the best Scottish land, and paid two fifths of the royal revenue.

And it was wise of the kings to have done this. The churchmen gave the kings their civil service and (through the pulpits of parish churches) a broadcasting service. The monasteries were welfare states which kept the country's schools, libraries and hospitals; they distributed poor-relief, and were the only organizations in which a labourer's son could grow more important than a landlord. Their buildings and lands were constructed, farmed and drained by the most modern scientific methods. From its foundation the Scottish Church had been patriotic, helping William Wallace in spite of kings and overlords; defying papal excommunication in the Declaration of Arbroath; wholly rejecting the idea that Canterbury and York Archbishops could control it. So Scottish kings had planted monasteries on the richest lands near the Scottish border. Jedburgh, Melrose and Kelso were buffers against English invasion, as well as centres of learning and sources of revenue. Christian armies were not supposed to attack Christian establishments on foreign soil. Edward the Hammerer had done it but Scotland and its monasteries had recovered from him.

Martin Luther demanded an end to the Roman Catholic Church in 1520; Henry VIII wrote a pamphlet defending the papacy for which the pope named him Defender of the Faith (a title still stamped on the coins of Elizabeth I of Britain) but after that Henry and the pope disagreed over a divorce case so Henry made himself pope of the English Church. Up till this time his spies and police had been discovering and burning Protestant heretics. They did not stop doing it, but started burning Catholic heretics too. Henry was a moderate, middle-of-the-road English king who impartially tortured and killed the extremists of every party who disagreed with him. Since many of his subjects were still Catholics he kept them down by giving the buildings, fields and farms of the English monasteries to his most loyal merchants, lawyers and civil servants. In a year or two the schools, libraries, hospitals and poor relief of the monastic welfare states were abolished and the commercial middle classes enriched. Two centuries later this class completely destroyed the power of the king.

How I wish Henry VIII had lived to see that! However, for a while he was very lonely. The Catholic kings of Europe formed an alliance against him while most Protestants thought it ridiculous that a worldly, money-grubbing king should appoint bishops and clergy – they had attacked the papacy because they thought it too worldly and money-grubbing. But Henry's best allies were money-grubbers. He suggested to the Scottish king and nobility that they too grab their Church's property because their Church had so much of it. Many nobles liked the idea, but not James V. He refused an alliance with Henry because he preferred to deal with France. Without declaring war Henry sent armies to conquer Scotland for him. They failed but they burned the Border towns and rich monasteries, and massacred the inhabitants. Big monasteries remained in the Highlands, Aberdeenshire and the central Scottish Lowlands. They remained until the Scottish people destroyed them.

For of course the Roman Catholic Church and its monasteries were corrupt institutions. They did indeed support
parasites whose lives were not Christian and gave little back
to the community for what they took from it. The history
of the Catholic Church is a history of reform movements:
Dominican, Franciscan and Jesuit orders, created to purify it
and make it more Christian, and which added to its strength.
The greatest Christian thinkers from the time of Italian Dante
to Dutch Erasmus had wanted to cleanse the papacy of worldly
power and the Church of its parasites. They never dreamed of
destroying the welfare states. By the 16th century, unluckily,
the only people with the strength to do the first had also the
greed and incentives to do the last.

We will never know how the Scottish Church would have
developed had Scotland kept its own government, but when
James V died in 1542 during another horrible English invasion
his daughter, Mary Queen of Scots, was less than a week old.
The English had garrisons in three Scottish forts upon the east
coast, garrisons provisioned from the sea – Scotland had no
Royal Navy to defeat them. Some Scottish lords saw that
English help would get them the Church's property. The only
safe place for the little queen was the court of France. She was
sent to Paris and the patriots in the Scottish parliament – the
biggest part – made Cardinal Beaton the nation's chancellor,
because he was head of an independent and highly patriotic
Church. So a small body of energetic reformers got inside his
palace in St. Andrews, murdered him, barred the doors and
called upon all true Scottish Protestants to arise and support
them. A teacher and former priest called John Knox did
so, but most Scots, reformers or not, were horrified by the
bloody lawlessness of the deed. The desperadoes were sincere
Christians of the sort who think those who disagree with them
are enemies of God, so murdering them is a charitable deed,
but they were also in English pay and had left Scotland with
no government but a horde of squabbling lords of whom some
were also secretly allied with the English.

But that is why the Independent Presbyterian Church of
John Knox took over Scotland. English rulers wanted it to.

Queen Elizabeth of England disliked Knox because he declared that female government was an abomination stinking in the nostrils of God. She financed and supported him in Scotland because he would destroy its links with France by destroying the Catholic Church there. An queen who ruled her Church through bishops, she supported a Calvinist demagogue who wanted every nation, including its monarch, ruled by a General Assembly of Protestant parish priests. It was a straight matter of international politics, like the Imperial German Government of 1917 (which hated Communism) sending Lenin into Russia so that the Communists would break the Russian alliance with France and Britain. English help in the founding of the Scottish Church has been obscured because the Scottish king who went to London became episcopalian too and tried to destroy the Church of Scotland – it practically destroyed them.

But John Knox's English helpers and supporters were well known to his Scottish clerical opponents, who said he was no true Scotsman and even wrote in a language like his English masters. One thing is certain: the Scottish people understood him. He was a great public speaker of the Hitler sort. Scottish lords could not take Church lands over while there were monks and their servants and serfs to fight back, but they easily occupied the rich leavings when Knox's sermons had excited crowds of Scottish townsmen to destroy the Church's buildings. "Burn the trees and the crows will fly," he explained, so the remaining Scottish monasteries with their schools and libraries, the great cathedral of St Andrews and the bits of the cathedrals containing schools and libraries were enthusiastically destroyed by many people who could not read or write anyway. Knox was not opposed to education; he wanted everyone in Scotland to be taught reading by his Calvinist priesthood, but the one book he wanted them all to read was the Geneva Bible which was mainly the work of English translators and immensely popular in England.

Knox was a man of admirable courage and honesty, horrible single-mindedness and cruelty. His *History of the Reformation in Scotland* is good pungent prose. He describes vividly the murder of Cardinal Beaton, calling it "merry work", and thinks it a splendid stroke of satire that afterwards a Protestant pissed in the corpse's mouth. He found it inconceivable that anyone who disagreed with him could be good or intelligent, but he was clever enough to see that the Scots lords who supported him had only done it for gain. He wanted the revenues of the Church lands given to his Calvinist priests who would build schools throughout Scotland, where the sons of labourers and landlords would sit side by side studying the word of God in Genevan English. He only partly got it. The Scottish lords rejected this stupid levelling idea. In his final years Knox knew the new lords of Protestant Scotland were worse than the old Catholics. The Catholic lords had supported a Church which pretended to help and educate the common people, the new lot helped nobody but themselves. They had used the Reformation to get the cheapest possible priesthood, a priesthood which governed nobody but the poor in a land which between the death of James V and the rule of his grandson James VI had no firm government for forty-one years – the five years of poor Queen Mary's rule spread instead of curbed the anarchy.

I suspect that in those forty years The Protestant Scottish Conscience (or Soul) was created. It resembles the Swiss Protestant conscience, and the Danish, and the Dutch for reasons given by Patrick Geddes in his description of the peasant character in poor countries, but the absence of a firm government, law-abiding landlords and a comfortable clergy made the Scottish soul a bleaker, less social thing. It is as if we had a small god in our brain who may sometimes sound like John Knox or a local schoolteacher but has nothing much to do with landlords, kings and such gentry. The demands of this little god are sometimes so severe that whenever he has been supported by clergymen of his own kind he has destroyed the happiness of whole communities, delighted in smashing church organs and sculptures, and revelled in the burning of poor old women; but Scots with radical new ideas who get their deity to co-operate with them have acted with courage and independence – the opposition or indifference of clergy, kings, bosses and nations has seemed trivial compared with their staunch self-approval. This god, soul, conscience or spirit made

William Paterson, a farmer's son, peddle a financial scheme which eventually ruined his nation through the money markets of Amsterdam, Berlin and London. It made David Livingstone prefer a lonely grave in central Africa to a living in Scotland, and made him famous as a great British missionary, though he only managed to convert one black man who afterwards changed his mind. It enabled John Maclean, the Glasgow schoolteacher who became Lenin's British Consul General, to scorn the British Communists who looked to Moscow for leadership. He died of pneumonia while attempting to found a Scottish Workers' Republic. It enabled . . .

Publisher: This is starting to sound like a flight of rhetorical fancy. Have a cup of tea and cool down.

Author: Certainly. Certainly.

CHAPTER 5

Emigrants

There were three brothers in merry Scotland,
In merry Scotland brothers three,
And they did cast lots which of them should go
For to turn robber all on the salt sea.

Scotland's thin soil meant that most Scots lived close to famine
so third sons – sometimes even second sons – often had to clear
out. In 1094 when the lords of feudal Europe prepared the first
crusade they were surprised to be joined by troops wearing
outlandish armour. These were Scots who had heard of the
crusade through their Church, but since they were outside
the feudal system the great lords had neither summoned
nor expected them. Another kind of Scottish emigrants were
scholars seeking education in European universities and jobs in
its Churches. They were tenacious people. Poverty had trained
them to live on little and grab the leavings of others, hence a
French saying that rats, mice and Scotsmen were to be found
everywhere.

After 1520 two centuries of warfare on the pretext of religion
ensured there was more money in fighting than scholarship.
Scottish privates, officers and generals fought for the king of
Sweden against the Danes, Poles, Muscovites and Germans;
for the king of Poland against Swedes, Muscovites and Turks;
for the Duke of Muscovy against Swedes, Turks and Tartars;
for the German emperor against Swedes, Dutch and Venetians;
for Dutch William of Orange against Spain and France; for
Philip of Spain against the Dutch and French; for Louis of
France against the Dutch and Spanish; and for Venice against
the Germans and Turks. Several who escaped mutilation and
death were given estates and foreign titles by the kings they
had served best; but the most rich, famous and successful

Scottish emigrant to profit by religious warfare was King James VI.

For forty-five years Queen Elizabeth had reigned in England and kept herself and her country free of political entanglements by not marrying – she enjoyed flirtation but was a resolute virgin. When she died the English Protestant Church, lords and parliament wanted a king who would not disturb their property, a Protestant king with no estates outside Britain, so they gave the job to Jamie. It is a pity he took it.

It is a great pity he took it. A king who dreaded warfare yet loved hunting, a pedantic scholar who doted on handsome young men but hated washing his hands, he had broken the power of the more lawless of his nobles using nothing but his wits and the help of people sickened by forty-one years of anarchic reformation. He had given them twenty years of central government but it had been a struggle and had not made him rich. When giving banquets to foreign ambassadors he had to borrow gold and silver plates from wealthier neighbours. Although Scottish trade had begun to prosper, although his people were grateful he was delighted to get away. It was much easier to rule Scotland from London.

Publisher: Are you going to tell me he was like the modern Scottish MP?

Author: Yes. In London he ruled England, Wales and Ireland too so felt much more important.

He now had a good civil service under him, a treasury and a House of Lords and bishops who let him be as extravagant as he liked as long as he protected their estates – and the only danger to these came from Ireland. The English had been conquering that land for centuries and it still troubled them. So Jamie bent his mind to the problem of Ireland.

The best way to exploit a land without living there is through tax farming. You make native rulers much richer by giving them more power to tax their subjects than they had without you, as long as their riches maintain the status quo – which is you, the conqueror. This only works in a land with a monetary system, and Ireland had practically none. Its trade was mostly barter, its taxes paid in goods and labour.

Another tactic is to find a native clan and isolate it from the others by paying it to work as your police force. Jamie and later British kings did that in the Scottish Highlands but it did not work in Ireland. The Irish persisted in hating the English more than each other, so Norman, Plantaganet and Tudor overlords had been forced to quell them by periodic massacres which left the winners sickened and exhausted, the Irish as Irish as ever. And the Irish were still Catholic! If English Catholics promised them more freedom they might send in an army by way of Ulster, crossing the narrow channel that divided it from the Scottish coast. It was from here the first Scots had left Ireland for Britain. A lot of English settlers could have held the country down, but English kings had persuaded hardly any English farmers to settle in the poorer land they would not visit themselves. Bearing all this in mind Jamie arrived at a tactic which could only be deployed by a Scottish king ruling Ireland with an English army: the colonization of Ulster.

This was the first and largest state-assisted emigration of Scots into another country. Two thirds of northern Ireland was confiscated by the British crown. The natives were ordered to leave or remain in the condition of servants, and their land was given to settlers from Britain – as long as they were Protestant. The great mass of these settlers were Scottish, of course. According to the English historian John Richard Green:

> In its material results the plantation of Ulster was undoubtedly a brilliant success . . . the foundations of the economic prosperity which has raised Ulster high above the rest of Ireland in wealth and intelligence were undoubtedly laid in the confiscation of 1610. . . . The evicted natives withdrew sullenly to the lands which had been left them by the spoiler; but all faith in English justice had been torn from the minds of the Irishry, and the seed had been sown of that fatal harvest of distrust and disaffection, which was to be reaped through tyranny and massacre in the age to come.

Green wrote that in 1874. He was referring to tyrannies and massacres in the 17th and 18th centuries, not the 20th. But with the backing of the Ulster Protestants the big Anglo-Irish landowners broke the power of the ancient clan chieftains and brought their land into the English mercantile system.

When King James (that royalest of emigrants) signed the act of confiscation he did not think he was splitting four nations into five, but joining them into one. He died in 1625 believing he had done it, but the civil wars which followed proved him wrong. Not only did rebellious English Catholics look for help from Ireland; rebellious English Protestants looked for, and got, military help from Scotland. The war which Cromwell won – the war between the English king and parliament – started in Scotland when the biggest number of the Scots lords and clergy rejected the king's order to accept bishops he had chosen and use prayer-books of the English sort. Then the English parliament found itself at war with Charles I on a matter of taxation, and the Scots offered aid in return for parliament making all England Presbyterian. The English parliament gladly accepted the aid but Oliver Cromwell never dreamed of forcing the Scottish system on English churches.

Two years after the English parliament had chopped off Charles's head the Scots crowned his son king of Great Britain at Scone and invaded the new English commonwealth with an army whose composition made no sense at all to the English. It contained royalist nobility who wanted Charles II to dominate the English parliament and Church once again, and Presbyterians who thought him a lever they could use to overturn the English Church absolutely. Cromwell utterly routed them. From the two or three thousand Scots taken prisoner the people of property were given a light prison sentence until ransoms were paid, the rest were sold and exported as slaves, chiefly to Barbados.

Sir Thomas Urquhart of Cromarty was one of the Scots defeated at Worcester. A royalist who disliked Presbyterians (the poorest part of the Scots army) he still thought that Christians selling other Christian into slavery was a new thing, at least in Britain. Perhaps; but this was the century which saw

the start of a competitive, commercial England which looked
to America, Africa and Asia. The slave trade greatly helped it.
The trade was in African blacks, many of whom passed through
Liverpool on their way to the New World. From 1651 to 1745
their numbers were swelled by the poorer class of Scot defeated
through battle in England, or Scotland itself.

By 1695 it was obvious to most Scots that having a king
in London had not benefited their country. Though Scotland
still had a parliament of lords and gentry they could only
deal with their ruler through a small number in the king's
pay. Meanwhile he signed English acts of parliament which
strengthened English colonies, English trade and the English
stock exchange in ways which excluded Scotland. English fleets
traded with colonies and plantations containing Scots slaves,
overseers and settlers, but excluded Scottish ships; nor could
the Scots trade freely with Europe because England was
usually at war with either Holland or France, her mercantile
and colonial competitors. When James VI had gone south over
ninety years before he had told the Scots he was going from
one part of an island to another to secure their greater comfort.
None had followed, except for some other clever emigrés who
went south too. William Paterson was the most successful. Here
is the entry on him in *Chambers Biographical Dictionary*:

William PATERSON (1658–1719), Scottish financier,
founder of the Bank of England was born at Skipmyre
farm, in Tinwald parish, Dumfriesshire, and spent some
years in the West Indies. Returning to Europe, he
promoted his Darien Scheme in London, Hamburg,
Amsterdam (where he worked for the Revolution of
1688) and Berlin, made a fortune by commerce in
London, founded the Hampstead Water Company in
1690, projected the Bank of England, and was one of its
first directors in 1694. At Edinburgh, as a strong advocate
of free trade, he talked the whole nation into his Darien
Scheme.

CHAPTER 6

More Emigrants

Paterson began by starting a Scottish Trading Company which (like the Bank of England in London) would be supported by the nation's parliament and finance its trade. On a globe of the world he proved that by planting a colony across the isthmus of Panama (Paterson told the Scottish parliament) their nation could create the most profitable trade route in the world. With ports on the Atlantic and Pacific shores Scots merchants could easily reach both coasts of North and South America, and open a route by way of the Pacific to Asia. This would destroy the monopoly of the East India Company without breaking a single English law. Moreover, the place was uninhabited. The king in London had recently passed a law saying his navy would protect British colonies planted on uninhabited coasts.

This scheme was so convincing that even London merchants joined it until the East India Company threatened to impeach them in the English parliament. The Darien Venture became wholly Scots. Lords, lairds, merchants and professional men became so patriotically hopeful that they invested half Scotland's money in Paterson's company – about £400,000 – of which they lost roughly £200,000. They should first have discovered why that part of Panama was uninhabited.

The Scottish emigrants sailed there and began building New Edinburgh, a port whose name never got printed on a globe of the world. The dank air was full of malaria. The settlers grew feverish soon after arriving, and had to fight off Spaniards who attacked them from a healthier part of the coast. When they asked their king in London for protection he said he could not give it because this would disturb the peace of Christendom. The Darien colony beat off the Spaniards once but eventually had to surrender. They begged help from nearby English colonies, who refused it. Paterson was one of the few hundred who got home, leaving about two thousand dead behind him and having lost a quarter of his nation's capital.

But he had done his best, so the Scots blamed the English. This was illogical. Mosquitoes had been the main enemy. The king in London had only been against the scheme because the London parliament rightly regarded him as their agent, not Scotland's. The families who ruled England had invited the Stuarts south because they thought the Stuarts would be more manageable than the other royal families available. They were mistaken. Taming the Stuarts had been a long, expensive struggle. As Alexander Pope said, "A king may be a tool, a thing of straw; but if he serves to frighten our enemies it is well enough; a scarecrow is a thing of straw, but it protects the corn." And the English grandees were not anti-Scottish racists. When Paterson founded the Bank of England with the help of the London parliament he was their partner. When he founded the Scottish Company with the help of the Edinburgh parliament he was their competitor. He had been foolish to think a British king would help the City of London's competitors. Then the City of London suddenly gave Scottish pride another hard knock.

Queen Anne came to the throne, the last of the Stuart monarchs since she was middle-aged and childless. Without consulting Scotland the English parliament decreed that the German Prince of Hanover would be King of Britain after her – he had promised to join the Church of England. The English parliament was as businesslike with its clergy as its kings. The big Protestant landlords paid the wages of their local clergy, choosing new ones from anybody they liked who had passed the easy exams of Oxford or Cambridge. This system appalled Scottish Presbyterians and Catholics alike. While hating each other they both believed that only their Churches should appoint their Churches' clergymen. Many of them had killed and been killed for that idea. So the Scottish parliament refused to recognize George Hanover as the next king of Scotland, and for a while it seemed Scotland would be independent again. The mass of the Scottish people wanted it. Probably the mass of the English people wanted it for they

certainly disliked the idea of a closer union. But democracy was
centuries away. . . . Are you listening to me, Stephanie?
Publisher: Yes. Why do you ask?
Author: Because I repeat, with emphasis, that the Scottish
people did not get the independence they wanted because
democracy was centuries away. It was the nobility who managed the two parliaments who dreaded the idea.

The English dreaded it because they had begun a trade war
with France which would last, on and off, until Napoleon
was sent to St Helena. Sharing a monarchy with Scotland
felt like a pain in the arse but an independent Scotland
would have felt like a knife at their back – the Scots would
probably have got in another Stuart king with French support. The Scottish lords and merchants now saw their only
hope of wealth through trade with England. One of them
(Fletcher of Saltoun) believed Scotland had the resources
to make herself a self-supporting republic, but the path he
suggested was strenuous and gave no chance of quick profit.
He wanted to abolish Scottish emigration by binding every
Scottish peasant to work on the estates where they were
born, while getting every landowner to employ and house
his estate workers using the newest scientific methods. His
advice was ignored of course. What most of the Scottish
parliament wanted was a new federal union with England
which would protect Scottish trade, in return for Scottish
loyalty to a new Anglo-German king. Scottish commission-
ers went to London to negotiate that in 1707. They failed.
They returned with a different treaty of union, the best they
could get.

It said that if the Scottish parliament would swear allegiance
to the German king the English would give them, and make
their revenue officers pay Scotland's taxes into the English government treasury, and abolish the Scottish Trading Company
(which still dealt with Africa) and then abolish itself, England's
parliament would allow Scottish parliamentarians:

45 SCOTTISH MPs ALLOWED TO JOIN 513 ENGLISH
AND WELSH MPs IN WESTMINSTER.

16 SCOTTISH LORDS ALLOWED TO JOIN 190 ENGLISH ONES IN WESTMINSTER.

ENGLISH PERMISSION FOR SCOTLAND TO KEEP ITS SEPARATE LAWS AND LEGAL SYSTEM.

ENGLISH PERMISSION FOR THE PRESBYTERIAN CHURCH TO BE THE OFFICIAL CHURCH OF SCOT-LAND.

AN IMMEDIATE CASH PAYMENT OF £398,085 AND 10 SHILLINGS.

This eccentric sum of money was supposed to equal Scotland's share of the debt (of overdraft) owed by the English government to the Bank of England, and which would become The Great British National Debt when the two parliaments joined. It certainly equalled the Scots investment in the Scottish Trading Company which owned the Scottish national debt and was to be abolished. This meant that Scottish shareholders would get back what they had lost on their Darien gamble.

During the long debate on this Treaty of Union an English government spy judged that the Scottish people were fifty-to-one against. Churchmen denounced it; burghs petitioned against it; Glasgow, Dumfries and Edinburgh mobs rioted against it. Most of the Scottish parliament hated it too, but dreaded the alternative. The English parliament had passed an Aliens Act, which would blockade Scottish trade if the Scots stayed independent. Beyond that lay a danger of warfare. England now had plantations and factories in Ireland, America, Africa and India. Without straining its credit it was fighting a successful war against France, the biggest nation in Europe. When that war was won it would certainly have a great enough army to crush an independent Scotland, would do it even more readily if it lost, and could easily find a pretext. It already had a precedent. In 1654 Cromwell had joined Scotland to England by conquest, ruling the northern nation with an occupying army until 1660. Scotland also had more recent experiences of civil war and English regiments.

This Treaty of Union promised the Scottish Parliamentary Lords peace, independence for their laws and Church, trade with England, a twelfth of the seats in a new Great British parliament, and money in their pockets. So among the curses of the nation that elected it, Scotland's independent parliament voted itself out of existence by a large majority.

The sixty-one lords and MPs who now represented their country migrated to London as a Scottish king had done a century earlier. The MP for the Dumfries Burghs, William Paterson, had worked hard to promote this Union since the failure of his Darien plan. Eight years later the Great British parliament awarded him £18,000 to compensate for what he lost in that. Though a bad colonizer he was still a financial genius.

Then the Independent Scottish Legal System discovered that in all but criminal matters the House of Lords over-ruled it. This allowed the British parliament to give big landlords the right to choose clergy for the Independent Scottish Church. Not all Scots clergy hated this – those who were chosen felt pleased – but it started a long turmoil in the Church of Scotland which eventually broke it in two. Meanwhile the British government spread taxation in a way which deliberately helped the English economy and depressed the Scottish. English coal could enter Ireland duty-free, Scottish coal could not. England's main industry was wool, and the government had a light export duty on it. Scotland's was linen, so the government put a heavy duty on it. Then English brokers took shares in the Irish linen trade, got a government subsidy to expand it, and began buying Scottish flax for it. Scots MPs protested that Scots law forbade the taking of flax from Scotland, since it would ruin the Scottish weavers. They declared that such acts broke the Treaty of Union. Here are replies they got from the Great British Government:

"Whatever are or may be the laws of Scotland, now she is subject to the sovereignty of England, she must be governed by English laws."

"Have we not bought the Scots and the right to tax them?"

"We have catcht Scotland and will keep her fast."

In his book *The Lion in the North* John Prebble says, "England's lack of sympathy for Scotland's particular needs seemed sometimes perverse and malicious, the triumphs of a small boy who is winning a game he has himself devised." He also says, "For more than a quarter of a century it did seem as if Union were a greater disaster than the Darien Venture."

But throughout the 18th and 19th and 20th centuries the British government encouraged one great Scottish industry: the export of people. An expanding and widespread financial empire needs continual supplies of soldiers. Since a working army uses up healthy men fast the British government could never have defeated the French in France, Canada and India with recruits wholly drawn from the poor and unemployed of South Britain, which was a comparatively prosperous place. It employed German and Irish mercenaries of course, but the language of the first and Catholicism of the second sometimes made difficulties for English commanding officers. But from Scotland, especially the Highland part, the British government was soon able to recruit whole regiments and their commanding officers too.

CHAPTER 7

Highland Disaster, Lowland Recovery

Publisher: Since you are obviously going to tell us about Bonnie Prince Charlie, Culloden et cetera you had better say something about Gaelic-speaking Scotland – the Scotland of the Highland clans. So far you have said more about the English, Irish and Ulstermen than them. Why?

Author: The lasting difference between Scotland and England seemed more important than a difference *inside* Scotland – a difference created by the split with the Catholic Church.

Publisher: But the difference between the Highlands and Lowlands is geology, not religion! You can see it on maps. Between Dumbarton and Aberdeen runs what they call The Highland Fault Line. North of it all the highest bens and deep glens and sea lochs begin. To English eyes the country to the south still looks on the wild side but it has a lot of broad valleys between much lower hills. It has all the broad coastal plains and nearly all the towns. I have also read enough to know the clansmen of the Highlands and Islands were fiercer warriors than the peasants and townsmen of the south, so John Knox did *not* invent the Highland Fault Line with English backing.

Author: True – but he and the Protestant ministers destroyed the Catholic ministry who had held the English-speaking south and Gaelic-speaking north-west and Scandinavian north together as a Scottish nation. Yes, the people of the glens and western islands depended more on hunting, fishing and cattle herding than on agriculture, but it was from the monastery of Saint Columba on Iona in the north-west that Scotland was Christianized. The Celtic Church was building abbeys in Scotland and Northumbria before Saint Augustine founded Canterbury, and while most of the English were worshipping Wodin and Thor. For centuries most people outside Britain thought the Scots and Irish were the same. Pelagius and Duns

Scotus were two of the greatest scholars to disturb and inform the Catholic Church – for a while all Rome and western Europe adopted the Pelagian Heresy, which insisted that the human will could rectify the disaster of the Fall. Pelagius and Duns Scotus lived six centuries apart and are claimed by both the Scots and Irish because they wrote in Latin and nobody now knows if they came from the west or east coast of the Irish Sea.

The great thing about these monks who used Jerome's Latin Bible and prayed in . . .

Publisher: Forgive my asking, but were your parents Catholics?

Author: (indignantly) Certainly not! My father was a Protestant atheist. My mother thought any church was a good social club if nobody in it took the religion seriously. I believe every religion in the world is absolutely true except when it fights with other ones; but my favourite religion is art – the speech, buildings, music, pictures, dramas and books we make for each other and to keep in touch with each other. I also like public houses, especially ones you can enter without paying at the door – libraries, cathedrals and art galleries, places created for everyone to share. I like the old Catholic Church because though its clergy used the international Latin language they also wrote the vernacular poetry and chronicles of their own people – the first literature of the Irish, Welsh and Anglo-Saxons.

Anglo-Saxon literature was forgotten (though not wholly lost) when William the Waster forced a different speech on the people. In Ireland and Wales Catholic clergy or patriotic, literate gentry lasted long enough to preserve some of the national literature. The wholesale destruction of the Scottish monasteries in the English-speaking and Gaelic districts of Scotland meant that practically no Gaelic vernacular literature has survived in Scotland from before the 19th century, when scholars of folk-lore began writing it down from Gaels who had learned the work of their greatest poets by ear and word of mouth. Both the Protestants and the Episcopalians who destroyed the Catholic Church in Scotland had declared the word of God could only be read in an English Bible, so Gaelic Christians were immediately outcast from the English-speaking Scottish Churches during centuries when they looked increasingly outlandish to first of all their king and then their parliament in London. No wonder many of the northern clans held to the Catholic faith! But clever Highlanders who wanted book learning had now to get it from the universities in Aberdeen, St Andrews, Edinburgh and Glasgow, which had once been cathedral schools but were now mainly training centres for a harsh Presbyterian theocracy whose prophet was John Calvin in Geneva.

So while the Scottish government was being broken off from Scotland, Catholic scholarship was cast out by Scottish schooling, and Highland and Lowland culture also got broken apart because Catholic clerics were evicted from Scottish schooling. However, they still had their local governments, the chiefs who lived among them: until after 1745.

Because the French were fighting the English on their own soil they put Prince Charles Edward (Sobiewski) Stuart (a half-Polish young man) on a Catholic part of the Highlands. Less than half the clans rallied to him. He entered Lowland Scotland and quickly defeated the small Hanoverian forces there and after enjoying some splendid parties in Edinburgh, where many elegant ladies loved him, marched into England. No Scottish Lowlanders were stupid enough to join him. Why should they exert themselves to put yet another king on the throne of England? The ones they had put onto it in the past had been unmitigated disasters for the Scottish people. When the Highlanders found no English were joining them either they sensibly went home. An English army followed and destroyed their army at Culloden, then butchered native civilians as a lesson to the rest, and arrested all who remained of the beaten army along with its probable sympathizers. Most of these prisoners were sold as slaves to America. However the main damage to Gaeldom was done through the clan chieftains approved by the British government.

Under the old Scottish laws the territory of each was equally the property of his people: if he was atrocious to them they could unite to get him replaced. The British parliament passed a law making the Highland "chieftains" the equivalent of English landowners – they could make money out of their bit

of Scotland in any way they pleased. In the 19th century this
sometimes meant driving their people out of glens and evicting
them to places like Canada since sheep were more profitable, or
later because they got higher rents from foreigners on hunting
holidays; but before this happened they made full use of the
old loyalty their men owed to them as military leaders. They
formed regiments, enlisted as colonels in the British army
and fought for England (for the south Britons kept thinking
of themselves as English) in France, Spain, America, Canada,
India et cetera. English generals found them excellent troops.
I will quote John Prebble again: "The last tragedy of the clans
may not be the slaughter of Culloden, but the purchase and
wasteful expenditure of their courage by the southern peoples
who had at last conquered them."

But while the Highlands were coming to terms with the
Great British government in the way I have described something more cheerful was happening in the Lowlands. The
disastrous thirty years following the Treaty of Union had
taught lairds, craftsmen and tradesmen there a good lesson:
they could only prosper by working together without the help of
a king, lords and parliament. They started doing what Fletcher
of Saltoun had advised, and made the Scottish Lowlands a
self-managing, middle-class republic, though one very alert
to all it could learn from other lands – including England.
They formed societies for the encouragement of land, trade
and science, but the scientific working of the land came first.
Two thirds of the farmed land in the Scottish Lowlands
was reclaimed from moorlands by drainage, manuring and
enclosures which began in the 18th century. Some of the
enclosures drove poor tenants off their soil, but much less of
this happened in Scotland than in England because in Scotland
new farms could be enlarged into uninhabited places. Scottish
landlords mainly working through Edinburgh lawyers leased
unproductive land at low rents to natives who would work hard
to make something of it. When they had done so the rents were
increased as much as possible. If the tenant could not pay the
higher rent he or his sons could be evicted to start work on
poorer soil again. The father of Robert Burns was a tenant

farmer of this kind. He and his son struggled from one poor
farm to another. Burns was eventually killed by the rheumatic
illness he had got at the age of twelve by overworking his heart
while helping his dad bring in a difficult harvest. Thousands
who were not great poets died early for similar reasons.

Yet Burns was a very great poet, and other geniuses came
from the Scottish tenant farmers and their small towns from
then till the early 20th century, though they were usually
scientists, inventors, doctors and explorers. There was nothing
of this in England, whose geniuses came from the prospering
middle classes. Meanwhile Edinburgh became one of the
capital cities of European intelligence, a centre of modern
civic architecture, philosophy and publishing, recognized by
Voltaire, Rousseau and Thomas Jefferson – the latter declared
that in scientific matters, "No place in the World can pretend
to a competition with Edinburgh."

This was helped by the increasing wealth of Glasgow in the
west. The winds let Clyde shipping reach America faster than
ships from other European ports. From their transatlantic slave
plantations Glasgow merchants brought back cotton, tobacco
and sugar, making fortunes which turned Glasgow into a
mighty capital city of industry – for a while. They were helped
by Scottish universities which gave a wider scientific training
to a much wider income range of students than could be got
at Oxford and Cambridge, whose main function was to train
Church of England clergymen and give a gloss of learning to
the sons of the very wealthy. It is not strange that the inventors
of the steam engine and gas lighting came from the west of
Scotland.

But for all that Scotland was a fractured nation.

Most British history books do not describe the Scots (and
Welsh, and Irish) as neighbours with lives as valuable and
complex as the English: they put them in isolated chapters
or paragraphs which fit into the book like ghettos into a big
city. Even David Hume and Thomas Carlyle – Lowland Scots
of very different mental tempers – wrote histories in which
Scotland appears like a northern slum whose voters sometimes
have to be pacified but which produces some queerly talented

people. They, like a certain facetious Church of England clergy-
man, saw Scotland as the knuckle end of Britain. Meanwhile,
histories of Scotland take the same kind of view: the Highlands
are presented like a northern slum tacked on to a highly
cultured Lowlands. There is a deal of truth in this view since
a lot of Scots have co-operated with the English to make it so.

CHAPTER 8

Democracy

In his *Lives of the English Poets* Dr Johnson, the most sensible
of English Tories, remarked that most nations are "formed
by accident and ruled by the passions of those who preside
in them." This is mainly true. Since the earliest nomads
covered the earth races have been defined by the natural
barriers of mountain range, sea coast and desert, which also
gave boundaries to nations created by conquest. A nation's
laws were therefore a set of traditional customs which helped
the natives survive, combined with a set of rules imposed by the
conquerors to help them keep control. Britain is an example of
this. It has never had a written constitution because the rulers
of the country know they could never agree to one, because they
would find it too inhibiting. There is a general agreement that
the freedom of the British people is guaranteed by our elected
parliament.

Before 1832 the electoral divisions of England and Wales
(where seven eighths of the British lived) were the same as
they had been when Edward, Hammerer of the Scots, had
authorized them in 1295. By the 18th century the English
people prided themselves as being the freest on earth because
one in every fifty could vote a member into the House of
Commons, and the king could do nothing without the support
of the Commons. Since whole towns had vanished since 1295
and new ones had grown up, several noble lords could choose
MPs without opposition and whole districts of folk were not
represented. This gave stability to the Tory or big land owners'
party. As seats were openly sold to the highest bidders this gave
stability to the Whig or city stock-brokers' party.

"This House is not a representative of the people of Great
Britain," said an MP who wanted reform. "It is the representative of nominal boroughs, of ruined and exterminated

towns, of noble families, of wealthy individuals, of foreign potentates."

Publisher: Who were the foreign potentates?

Author: Maybe the Hanoverian kings (who also rigged the system to put in their own MPs) but perhaps the nabobs. A nabob was a merchant who had made a fortune in India. In a book called *The Member Galt* (who knew the type well) describes a Scottish nabob who decides to enter parliament so that he can give jobs to his hungry relatives. He finds Scottish parliamentary seats cost too much because Scotland's political managers are a few noble families who charge too high for their seats. To get one cheaply he buys votes from the councillors of an English county town. People who disliked the idea of political reform never denied the corruption. They said it was "as notorious as the sun at noonday", and a bastion of British liberty, whose main enemy was the greatest part of the British people – "the swinish multitude", as one parliamentarian called them.

This was the style of the government which ruled Ireland with an army and tried to rule North America with one. The Americans defeated it after a five years' war and made a government of their own. Having broken away from an accidental or historically accumulated political system, the United States leaders had to deliberately make one by writing down a governing constitution. This had not been done since the days of ancient Greece and Rome. They created a democratic system to ensure that every American could vote for their government – except women, children, slaves and the country's original inhabitants. History showed them that democracy's worst enemies are big hereditary lords, so they decreed that no United States citizen should have a hereditary title or wear official robes which made them look grander than others. Some farmers and tradesmen argued that not titles and robes but huge inherited fortunes were the essence of lordship: they urged that the Constitution limit the size of the fortune a citizen could make or inherit, to stop future USA governments being manipulated by cliques of rich men and their families, as in Britain. But the rich estate owners who had led resistance to Britain decided that the pursuit of unlimited wealth was essential to United States democracy; so it is, to this day.

But while the Yankees were making their own kind of federal nation they accidentally turned Britain into one also. To fight a futile war across the Atlantic the British took most their troops out of Ireland and, to stop it rebelling too and hold it for the British king, allowed middle-class Protestant Irish to elect a parliament of their own which sat in Dublin. It represented a nation which was over 90% Catholic and peasant; yet the American example led it to show remarkable independence from the parliament in London. Its leaders spoke out for Catholic representation. And in mainland Britain the slogan "no taxation without representation" made sense too. Party leaders in the Commons, tired of obstruction from MPs planted there by the king and lords, called on the unrepresented middle class to form *Societies of the Friends of the People*, to whip up support for parliamentary reform among the multitude. Then the French nation (whose government was hereditary and whose upper class never paid taxes) went bankrupt and . . .

Publisher: Stop stop stop! What about *SCOTLAND?*

Author: I cannot explain why a British government promised Scotland its own elected parliament in 1896 – but did not give it – and another in 1979 – and did not give it – unless I go back to France.

Publisher: O please don't try to summarize the French Revolution.

Author: I won't, but I will quote what Carlyle wrote after describing the start of it; the peaceful harmonious start when deputies of the Third Estate (the People) marched to Notre Dame Cathedral to celebrate what everyone knew was the start of a new era.

Yes, friends, ye that sit and look, bodily or in thought, well may ye look for it is a day like few others. It is the baptism day of Democracy. A superannuated System of Society is now to die; and so, with death-throes and birth-throes, a new one is to be born. What a work, O Earth and Heavens, what a work! Battles and blood-shed, September Massacres, retreats from

Moscow, Waterloos, Peterloos, Tenpound Franchises, Tarbarrels and Guillotines; and from this present date some two centuries of it still to fight! Two centuries; hardly less; before Democracy go through its baleful stages of *Quackocracy*; and a pestilential World begun to grow green and young again.

Carlyle was describing an event in 1789 from his standpoint in 1835 when most middle-class reformers believed Britain had at last got all the democracy it needed. MPs for new industrial cities sat in Westminster, MPs for non-existent towns had vanished; moreover, everyone who paid ten pounds a year or more in rates was entitled to vote, which meant that company shareholders could choose MPs but not any factory workers, rich farmers but not their labourers. The Irish parliament had been abolished because in the late war with France it had acted more independently than the English parliament could stand, so now some Irish Protestant MPs sat in Westminster. The French had a national education system brought in under Napoleon; the British would have none before 1870 because it was a burden on the taxpayer, and most MPs thought too many working men were reading political books, writing petitions about their grievances and forming trade unions – which were illegal. There was widespread unemployment and poverty; infectious diseases periodically spread to the politer parts of cities from overcrowded, foully drained, jerry-built slums. The cure for it all (nearly everyone but the suffering classes believed) was to send surplus Britons out to the healthy plains of Canada and Australia.

That is why Carlyle saw that democracy must struggle through many sham forms of itself before triumphing around 2035 AD. I hope he is right. It means I will see it if I live to be a hundred.

Publisher: But surely the 1832 Reform Bill was not a total sham? If it increased the voters from one in fifty to one in thirty it surely did some good?

Author: Yes, and so did the legalization of trade unions which allowed skilled workmen some voice in the government of their

wages, hours and workshop. So did Municipal Corporations·
which allowed more people a say (however little) in the government of their cities, because before the 19th-century ended
most British people lived in cities. But generally speaking the
improvement of living standards in the 19th-century cities was
the work of businessmen who needed well-made, well-lit streets
to do business in, clean drinking water and sewage systems
because the diseases of the poor could infect the rich, and whole
new classes of literate, self-respecting clerks and workmen to
help market their goods and make their machinery. It was to
get more skilled working-class helpers on their side that the
vote was extended to all but the very poorest men in 1867. And
in Scotland . . .

Publisher: (thankfully) At last!

Author: I had better start a new paragraph.

In Glasgow, Paisley, Dundee, Kirkaldy and other small
burgeoning industrial towns business went briskly between
the slumps. The coal-mines and iron-fields supplied them
with raw materials, Scottish colleges and universities supplied
them with engineers, and housed scientists whose discoveries in
mechanics and electrical science were of immediate use to their
countrymen as well as internationally. From the farmlands and
fishing ports the railways took a wealth of nourishment to
the always expanding market of London. The housing and
work conditions for the lowly paid was far worse than for
the equivalent social group in England. The big towns had
the cheap labour pool of the Highlands and Islands to keep
the wages down. When the handloom weavers demonstrated
against the destruction of their industry, when the cotton
weavers demonstrated against a reduction of wages, banners
were waved on which the name of Wallace was inscribed
beside the local radical leader; but the well-doing folk felt
smugly proud of Scotland's place in the mighty British Empire,
whose Scottish regiments with kilts and pipes added drama
to Crimean, Indian and African battle scenes shown in *The
Illustrated London News* and civic art galleries. Intricate monu-
ments to Walter Scott, Robert Burns, William Wallace and the
Scottish victims of imperial battles arose in the land, but no

hint of the number of natives they slew in the native homeland. And the queen spent half her life on Deeside, and most of the British cabinet spent two or three weeks on a Scottish grouse moor or salmon river or golf course during recess. Toward the end of the century the British Admiralty started ordering its battleships from Clydeside instead of Thameside, and some London newspapers printed panicky articles about The Drift of Industry to the North. An arms race with Germany had begun. The British Imperial War Department drew up plans for a deep-water canal from the Clyde to the Forth by way of Flanders Moss. Imagine the huge Dreadnought destroyers sailing back from the North Sea between the Wallace Monument and Stirling Castle! What a sight it would have been!

Publisher: But . . . they would have to go through Loch Lomond.

Author: Exactly! Loch Lomond would have become the biggest inland harbour and refitting base for the greatest navy the world had seen, its shores and islands covered by mighty forges and cranes . . .

Publisher: Is this one of your fantasies?

Author: No. It was a fantasy of the British Imperial War Department.

Publisher: You started off talking about democracy.

Author: It is not easy to talk about democracy and Scotland simultaneously in the 19th century. But some of it suddenly happened where no prophet, and certainly not Karl Marx, would have dreamed of it. Crofters in the Western Isles – part of the Gaelic Scotland which laws and landowners from the English-speaking rest of Britain were pressing toward extinction – successfully counter-attacked – got the laws of Britain changed in their favour for a while – and nearly gave Britain the political constitution she will have in 2035 AD, if Carlyle's prediction comes true.

Publisher: You *must* be fantasizing now.

Author: No, just exaggerating. What they actually obtained – and what they did not quite obtain – came from copying the Irish when the Liberals were in power.

Since the Tories in those days were still the main party of the big landowners it was they who usually passed laws improving the conditions of the factory workers at the expense of the bosses. The Liberals, being based where the heavy industries were, liked winning votes in the country by passing laws that pleased the rural workers. Ireland had few heavy industries and was mainly farmed by cottagers like the Scottish crofters: liable to eviction if they could not pay rents in a bad year, or if their landlord found a more profitable use for the ground than letting natives live on it. Davitt the Socialist Catholic, Parnell the Protestant, were Irishmen who wanted home rule, and Parnell was chief of most Irish MPs in the House of Commons. They had organized the tenants and villagers to resist eviction, withhold unfair rents and boycott those who tried to enforce it. This example was exactly what the Scottish crofters wanted. They followed it. On the Isle of Skye the people of a small crofting village refused to leave their homes when an eviction notice was served on them. They drove off the local policemen, then a detachment of police sent from Glasgow. On the Island of Lewis a thousand folk with pipes and flags raided a sheep farm where their ancestors had lived, and were beaten back by soldiers of the Royal Scots brought in by HMS *Jackal*. And then (which shows why votes matter) a Crofters Party was formed, which in 1896 returned four MPs after a general election.

This was the year when Mr Gladstone introduced a bill which, if passed and implemented, would have created the United States of Britain, with separate parliaments for Ireland, Scotland, Wales and England.

CHAPTER 9

The Scottish Archipelago – Some Light Relief

In 1983 I was phoned by a man who said, "My name is Jacques Duras. I am French. I have come to Scotland to make a film about Scotland. I have read your novel *Lanark* which deals with Glasgow and would like you to take part in this film. Can I visit you to talk about this?"

I said he could so he did. He was a brisk, sparely built, efficient professor who had lectured on French writing at Edinburgh University and now lectured on Scottish writing at Montpellier. Two anthologies of his translations from Hugh MacDiarmid and other modern Scottish poets had been published in France and were used by French teachers. He said the film he was directing was an educational documentary and no one would make money by it. His technicians and equipment belonged to a student film unit; however they worked to a high professional standard and he hoped to get a wide distribution because the French are interested in Scotland. For historical reasons many of them preferred it to England, though not all of them understood the nature of the difference nowadays. He believed his film would elucidate the difference. He thought it not remarkable that a professor from Montpellier should be making the film. The University had a Patrick Geddes Society – a society of thinkers devoted to the ideas of that very great Scottish scientist and philosopher: also Jules Verne was buried in Montpellier under a strangely carved tombstone, and Verne had set two of his scientific romances in Scotland (*The Green Ray* and *The Child of the Cavern*) for obvious reasons.

It is interesting to see ourselves from a stranger's viewpoint, for even if the view is a friendly one it usually comes as a surprise. Clemenceau, defending the outsider's view of things once asked, "Who knows more about Lake Geneva? I who have walked round the shore, or the fish who swim in it?"

My own answer would be, the fish of course. Lake Geneva is their world. It surrounds them on every side. They swim through it and it flows through them so only they know exactly how it tastes. On the other hand Clemenceau can see the streams flowing in and out and many fish never notice these. If the loch is polluted by sewage from a nearby town Clemenceau may know the cause of something the fish take for granted, because they have grown used to polluted water. Again, if the fish live in shoals which keep to their own bays instead of swimming about and mingling, Clemenceau may notice a rare fish ignored by the shoals. Few Scots and very few Britons have heard of Patrick Geddes. I first learned of him in a book by Lewis Mumford, the American critic and social theorist, and at first thought Mumford had invented him, he sounded so improbable. However, reference books prove he really existed though they describe him differently. Born in 1854 he became Professor of Botany at Dundee, then Professor of Civic Studies in Bombay. *Everyman's Encylopaedia* says he was a scientist who co-authored *The Evolution of Sex* in 1890 and published *Cities in Evolution* in 1913. *Chambers Biographical Dictionary* says, "He threw himself with energy into schemes of town planning, Celtic publishing, and social, academic and economic reform." The most thorough recent account of him is in Duncan Macmillan's history of Scottish art, but even Macmillan does not mention that Geddes designed Tel Aviv, the layout of Edinburgh Zoo and was architect of Ramsay Gardens, Edinburgh University's first hall of residence which (long since privatized) overlooks the Esplanade of Edinburgh Castle. He also added several words to the English language, the best known being "conurbation". He used it to define modern industrial places (like Glasgow) which he said were neither towns or cities in the old sense of these words, but collections of them which needed new systems of government to manage them. It was disturbing that a French professor thought so highly of a Scot the Scots hardly knew, but I did not discuss that. Instead I asked him what obvious reasons had led Jules Verne to set two scientific romances in Scotland.

Scottish culture impressed the French most strongly in the

hundred years which followed the defeat of the '45 rebellion, and in two completely different ways. Edinburgh was then the main centre of the British book trade outside London; and contained the biggest group of philosophers, natural, social and historical philosophers to gather in one small British city, along with some effective publishers. The *Encylopaedia Britannica* was first printed here beside the works of Hume, Reid, Robertson and Adam Smith. In his autobiography Edward Gibbon quotes with pleasure a letter from David Hume complimenting him on the first volume of *The Decline and Fall of the Roman Empire*. Hume told him that the intellectuals of Edinburgh had been astonished to see that an Englishman was still capable of writing a work of genius at a time when most Englishmen preferred to concentrate on the puerilities of party politics. Many Londoners of distinction and authority had an equal contempt for the Scottish literati who were far more highly regarded in Paris. Dr Johnson, one of the greatest English writers, disliked them because they were too sceptical to have much faith in Christian churches.

James Macpherson published *Fingal, an Epic Poem in Six Books* in 1762 which he claimed to have translated from the Gaelic. It described a dim, heroic world of love, battles, swords and sorcery among the mountains and glens of the north. To most modern readers it would seem a very long, dank and foggy poem, but 18th century readers were growing tired of poems which were long, neat and very, very dry, so it struck many of them like a breath of fresh air. It rapidly went through many editions. The French translation was even more popular than the English original. Napoleon loved it. Before his career took off he wrote a long poem of the same kind, but no publisher would look at it. When Emperor he commissioned paintings based on the Macpherson poem, and had Malmaison deco-rated with a vision of Ossian, the Homer of ancient Scotland, inviting soldiers killed in Napoleon's battles into the cloudy heights of a Gaelic Valhalla.

So the French were simultaneously impressed by two ideas of Scotland, one plain, sceptical, rational and scientific, the other tremendous, heroic and weird: and as Scotland moved through the Industrial Revolution into the 19th century this double image was reinforced. Watt who invented and marketed the steam engine, Murdoch who invented gas lighting, were contemporaries of Walter Scott whose poem *The Lady of the Lake* brought tourists by thousands to view Loch Katrine and the Trossachs, and started the Scottish tourist industry. The poem described a Scottish king lost in the Highlands and his adventures with the daughter of an outlawed Highland chief whose hide-out is a wooded island; yet in 1859 Queen Victoria crossed the loch on the steamer *Rob Roy* to the the mouth of a seventeen-mile-long tunnel. Here she turned a handle which turned Scotland's most romantic body of water into what was then the largest municipal reservoir of pure water in the world. It belonged to Glasgow, which in that year and for a few years after was the world's single biggest producer of industrial machinery. Scotland was broadcasting such conflicting messages about the nature of its people that foreigners could not help being fascinated. When the Industrial Revolution got under way even the Scots were unable to imagine Scotland as a whole. Scott had shown the interdependence of Highlander and Lowlander in *Waverley* and *Rob Roy*, but had set these novels in the 18th century. No imaginative thinker even attempted to do the same during the huge industrial growth of the 19th. The only attempt at it is one of Verne's silliest novels, *The Child of the Cavern*, which describes the creation of an underground mining town in the heart of the Trossachs. Lit by electricity and completely insulated from the horrors of the Scottish climate, it is linked by railway to Edinburgh where the owner lives, and the owner and his workers talk together in mutual friendship and trust.

Jacques Duras' explanation of how Frenchmen from Napoleon to Jules Verne had viewed Scotland was not as ironical as my summary of it, perhaps because the French take paradoxes in their stride. I asked him how he would bring this vision up to date. He told me that in his view modern Scotland was not a country but an archipelago – a collection of islands, though most of the islands were not separated by water. Not only were the Orkneys and Hebrides spiritually and

economically separate from each other and the mainland;
Edinburgh, Glasgow, Dundee and Aberdeen were equally
separated from each other and from the farming counties,
the fishing ports, the mining villages, and industrial towns
like Bathgate, Linwood and Motherwell. He could not, of
course, show all of this in his film but would indicate it
by filming four places with a writer from each answering
questions about it. Iain Crichton Smith for the Western Isles,
George Mackay Brown for Orkney, Norman MacCaig for
Edinburgh and Alasdair Gray for Glasgow. Such a film, he
thought, could teach France a useful lesson, because France
was over-centralized – too dependent upon Paris. Scotland was
an example of a nation in good working order though without
a government of its own.

I have not quoted Jacques Duras because of his film but
because of his vision of Scotland as an archipelago, which
strikes me as true: hideously true although we are not a
nation in good working order. We are not even a province
in good working order. Since 1890 the fact that Scottish
health, housing, wages and employment are much worse than
in south Britain has been so obvious that, except in times
of warfare, it has always been tabled for discussion by the
London parliament which, unfortunately, has always had more
important things to debate. I will talk of this later. Meanwhile,
to end this chapter on a hopeful note, I will do so with a story
from Scottish working life. Unluckily it is from working life in
the luxury trade, because the workers I speak of are poets and
novelists, people as unnecessary to the good of a country as its
journalists and restaurateurs.

In the mid-1980s James Kelman was employed by Renfrew
Public Libraries to organize a writers' festival and he invited
to it writers from the islands of Glasgow, Edinburgh, Skye and
Lewis. For a day or two we ate, slept, read and conversed in the
Rockfield Hotel, and there was at first some friction of a sort
which often happens when people from different clans come
together. As usual the greatest friction was between the closest
neighbours: in this case the Glaswegians and Edinburghers.
Since the 1930s the best *group* of poets in Scotland had lived in

Edinburgh. Goodsir Smith, Garioch and MacCaig lived there. MacDiarmid was sometimes identified with them, though in his discordant way MacDiarmid belonged to the whole land. Born and educated in a Border weaving town he became a journalist in an eastern seaport, lived on a Shetland croft, became an industrial worker in Glasgow, and ended his days in a Lanarkshire farm cottage; but the Edinburgh poets were latterly his closest friends. Shortly before this festival, however, some Glasgow writers had been noticed by the public. Norman MacCaig in his slow, quiet voice and with a V-shaped smile remarked upon the Glasgow literary Mafia and I (being one of these) lost my temper and pointed out that Edinburgh was to blame for public attention to the prose writers among us. Our first novels and short stories, though written in Glasgow, had been published by Edinburgh firms. MacCaig was amused but not, I think, displeased. Everyone became friendly after that and the Gaels who were present had most to do with this. Since there is no Highlands and Islands university Sorley MacLean was educated at Edinburgh University, Iain Crichton Smith at Aberdeen, Angus Nicolson and Catriona Montgomery at Glasgow. That they were equally friendly with all of us made it possible for us to be equally friendly with each other. The differences between our urban and country backgrounds became a matter of fruitful conversation, not a gulf dividing us.

The next time we came unexpectedly together was in a set of readings supporting the miners in the strike of 1985. Most well-known Scottish writers took part in these. I had not expected this. Since MacCaig was from Edinburgh and his accent struck my ear as upper-class I had thought MacCaig would be against the miners – I give that as an example of the stupid prejudice which develops in a split-apart land. Of course it was easy for writers to support the miners, because we could do it without going on strike.

The Scottish steel workers could only have supported the miners by going on strike, but that would have put at risk the feeding, clothing and housing of their families; besides, the Tory government might have used a Scottish steel workers' strike as an excuse for shutting the Scottish steel industry down,

as it finally decided to do seven years later. The leader of the
steel workers announced that he could not ask his people to
sacrifice themselves for the miners, so the isolated miners were
defeated and now on the Scottish mining islands the quality
of feeding, clothing and housing has become far, far worse
because what was once Britain's strongest union has hardly
any strength left at all. So now (in March 1992) the steel island
of Motherwell has no strong allies. The Scottish National Party
has promised it will keep the place working but could only do
that if most voters in our archipelago put it into power.

Meanwhile I cannot help thinking the loneliest, most insulated Scots of all are the seventy-two Scottish MPs on the
neighbouring island of England. They are the second largest
tribe in a parliament of five hundred and twenty-three English,
thirty-eight Welsh and seventeen Ulstermen. How remote and
far away the islands they represent must appear to them. They
are surrounded by a city containing more people than Scotland,
Wales and Ulster put together. The six hundred and fifty
inhabitants of Westminster are strong and, for the most part,
secure. Their treasury is filled by taxes drawn from every part
of the United Kingdom, except the Channel Islands which,
being part of Britain but self-governing, have no members of
parliament so are useful tax havens for English millionaires.
But the treasury is still rich and out of it our six hundred
and fifty chosen leaders must support the industry, encourage
trade, and keep the peace in all these islands. How much do
the Scots put into the treasury and how much do they get back?
Nobody can say. In 1950 a Government committee was set up
to determine the true financial arrangements between England
and Scotland. The committee announced that the task was
impossible. Meanwhile every Englishman knows that Scotland
contains miles and miles of nearly empty moorlands, coasts
and islands, good ground for building nuclear power-stations,
storing nuclear weapons, disposing of toxic wastes.

Since the 18th century sculptors and political cartoonists
have often represented nations as single people, usually robust
and beautiful women with names like La France, Italia,
Germania. If Scotland were so depicted the head would

have to be shown attached to the body by a longer neck than the poor lady's height; moreover the head would also be attached by a neck of normal length to a different and much stronger body. No wonder many Scottish limbs and organs are underfed, numb and disconnected from each other. Too many of them cannot act without orders from a remote head which is distinctly absent-minded toward them because it must first direct a far more urgent set of limbs and organs.

CHAPTER 10
Sorts of Future

I hope the difference between the last chapter and the one
before it provoked thought. Chapters 2 to 8 swiftly sketched
how a nation was made, damaged, lost its government and
survived without, until the more fertile and industrial part was
in a state of confident Victorian activity, being a busy partner in
the biggest territorial empire the world has known. Yet in that
high imperial noon the demeaned and neglected people of the
north-west – the folk who had gained nothing from the part-
nership – acted independently (and illegally!) to get laws made
which would secure their homes for them. They succeeded
in this and more than this, being part of an independence
movement in Wales and Ireland too. A bill was presented to the
House of Commons to give Scotland (and Wales, and Ireland)
a government inside its own boundaries again. The bill was
presented by Liberals who mainly represented the industrial
cities, but was supported by Irish MPs, the four Crofters Party
MPs, and the Independent Labour Party headed by Keir
Hardie, journalist and ex-coalminer. Most supporters of the
bill also wanted the break-up of the big private estates covering
most of Britain. The Tory Party opposing the bill were also, of
course, defending the big private estates, and had a permanent
majority in the House of Hereditary Landlords.

The bill was passed by a majority of ten. Since the reader
knows it was never enacted Chapter 9 stopped being historical and went personal, sketching Scotland now from the
standpoint I know best – that of a worker in one of the
few Scottish trades in a healthier state than at the start of
this century: the imaginative writing division of the luxury
trade, in which Gael and Sassenach are not divided, yet
from which Scotland seems a heap of disconnected parts in
a steadily worsening state. Nobody will deny my description

of the present state. I will try to sketch rapidly how it was reached.

The alliance which passed the bill did not last, for the Nationalists and Land Nationalizers in it broke the Liberals up. The Liberal Unionists formed a party which sided with the Tories; yet the Liberal alliance achieved one great thing before the Labour Party MPs outnumbered it, creating Old Age Pensions so that the aged poor had a chance to die in their homes instead of the poor-house. This luxury was part of a Social Insurance scheme funded by worker and employer too, but also by Death Duties on the big estates. This was the foundation of the British Welfare State and Tory hatred of it; though Germany had possessed one since Bismarck's day. Winston Churchill was Liberal Home Secretary then. In 1910 he offered to implement the earlier bill by creating parliaments for Scotland, Ireland and Wales with seven English regional councils. He was given the Admiralty.

Then came the Great War which wrecked and reshaped millions of lives and altered the character of British politics. The Irish had been promised political independence when the war had started, but some of the leaders did not believe that promise because it had been given and broken before. In 1920 most of the Irish elected a parliament without asking Great Britain's permission. Civil war started and the main part of Ireland, by getting out of the British Empire, did what the USA had done in 1784 when it fought clear: it created a Federal Britain, giving Ulster an independent parliament of its own with its own separate constitution and heads of state departments. Meanwhile in Scotland the small but growing Nationalist Party was being mocked for wanting such things.

But in Scotland the difference from England was also being asserted by the Independent Labour Party. Its programme was still Land Nationalization, independent governments for the British nations, and an international workers' strike to stop warfare. This programme had been mainly discarded by the British Labour Party. The ILP had created that, but Clydeside was almost the only part of Britain that returned Independent Labour MPs. They were the radical part of the Labour Party, the part that wanted more socialism than the others thought possible. Local government housing for the working classes, free milk for under-nourished children was . . .

Publisher: (frantically) Do you realize it is 7.45 am on Monday the 16th of March? Do you realize the text of this book *must* be given to the printers before 12 noon in Edinburgh? And you are still in Glasgow? You've got to wrap it up fast. Say quickly why Scotland is in such a bad way nowadays. Why do you think life in Scotland is getting worse for most people?

Author: Because life for people in Britain is getting worse, except for those where capital is working – in the City of London, and the pieces of Britain its bankers and brokers want to invest in. Big money likes centralizing industry. If (or when) Ravenscraig shuts, the British steel industry will be centred in South Wales. Good for the Welsh! But finance is international, fast moving and continually shifting to more profitable centres. The Welsh steel industry may be a halfway house in shifting all British industrial investment to Germany. Why not? London finance, channelled through the government, made Scottish industry dependent on both when it ordered the warships from the Clydeside yards. There was bound to be a slump when the war stopped. The slump did not affect most owners of Scottish industry, who had made enough out of the war to live on it. They honestly told the Scottish industrial workers that they could not employ them or pay good wages until the British government gave them orders. That is why the Scottish Independent Labour Party went to London and eventually became the sort of Labour Party which now prevails in Scotland – a servile follower of the London government, whether Labour or Tory.

The Clydeside Independent Labour MPs who joined the British Labour Party, hoping to make it more socialist and independent, were a bit like the Scottish Protestants who supported Cromwell because they thought his parliament would create a Presbyterian Britain. The Clydeside MPs helped Britain as a whole to get a bit more social welfare between the wars, but no more than the Liberals would have created had they stayed strong. Some kinds of Tories saw the sense in that sort of thing too. But not nowadays. Nowadays the Labour leadership sees the sense of what the Tories do . . .

Publisher: (loudly) What party will you vote for in the next election?

Author: On every big disagreement between the Labour and Tory Parties from the CND to the Poll Tax, the Labour leaders in the London parliament have sided with Tories. Look at the Kilbrandon Report! Government committees had been reporting on the poor state of Scotland since the 1950s, each urging more independence for Scotland as the best aid for it, and in 1974 Kilbrandon advised not only a Scottish parliament, but the British constitution suggested by the 1894 Liberal bill, and which Churchill had been eager to implement in 1910. And both Labour and Tories denounced it. And when Scottish Nationalist successes and the local Labour parties forced a Labour government to hold a referendum in 1979, the Labour and Tory leaders both appeared on television saying, "Don't vote for a separate government! Only a single strong British government can defend you! If you don't vote for it even more capital will be withdrawn from Scotland, more industries will close, there will be a huge increase in unemployment." In spite of which a Scottish majority chose separate government. But we did not get it, because the Labour Party ruled that the race must be won by a head and neck, not half a head. No, we did not get it, and after that even more capital was withdrawn from Scotland, more industries closed, unemployment increased.

Publisher: Will a separate Scottish parliament improve things?

Author: I think Scottish poverty will get worse whether we have a Scottish government or not. I think it almost certain that the London government will regard an independent Scottish one as an excuse to strip assets from this country even more blatantly. I also think a new Scottish parliament will be squabblesome and disunited and full of people justifying themselves by denouncing others – the London parliament on a tiny scale. But it will offer hope for the future. The London parliament has stopped even pretending to do that. I believe an independent country run by a government not much richer than the People has more hope than one governed by a big rich neighbour.

Publisher: But a poor government is likely to be bribed.

Author: Yes, the People will have to watch it closely. But that will be easier to do when we surround it.

Publisher: And what kind of Scotland would you like to see happening?

Author: One where Scots mainly live by making and growing and doing things for each other. It should be possible. We have the room to do it.